I Sing of Hope

Valdir R. Steuernagel

A division of World Vision International
121 East Huntington Drive
Monrovia, California 91016-3400 USA

I Sing of Hope

Valdir R. Steuernagel

Scripture quotations are taken from the HOLY BIBLE: NEW
INTERNATIONAL VERSION. Copyright © 1973, 1978,
1984, by the New York International Bible Society. Used by
permission of Zondervan Bible Publishers.

ISBN: 0-912552-82-4

Published by MARC, a division of World Vision International, 121 East Huntington Drive, Monrovia, California
91016-3400, U.S.A.

Printed in the United States of America. Editors: Edna Valdez
and Jack Kenyon. Interior page design: Edna Valdez. Cover
photo: David Ward.

Contents

Introduction

THIS LITTLE BOOK has a story attached to it. Telling stories is possibly the only way I know how to write. When we look at our stories in the light of the stories in Scripture, our whole lives are touched by a radical call to discipleship. And we will never be the same.

I was in the middle of my theological studies, and I was worried. After two years of preaching, I thought I had said everything relevant that I could imagine.

I went to share this concern of mine with an experienced pastor. He was helpful. "You know," he told me, "what happens is that the biblical text always speaks to us in a different way. And we always come to the text in a different way. The continuous encounter between us, our context and the Word of God is one of the most fertile encounters I know, and a very exciting one as well."

The psalm that I liked most was the twenty-third. Almost everyone in our Christian tradition knows it and has some experience with it. I did. Then two things happened in my life and I discovered, read and reread Psalm 146.

First, I found out that the gospel has a special way of touching and committing people and communities in their totality. The gospel has a way of entering our everyday experience and conversing with it, changing it, without compartmentalizing and dichotomizing our human experience.

Second, I received a challenge to open my eyes and see what happens in the world, whether from the micro or macro perspective. Life, after all, goes on far beyond my existence and concerns. The church, in its turn and as the people of God, is called to go far beyond the walls of its buildings, structures and doctrinal formulations. Discipleship, I concluded, is kingdom business. The kingdom of God eagerly pushes to become real not only within the church but also in the world. Our commitment to the kingdom, in turn, drives us toward being a transforming presence in the world.

In the middle of this whole process, Psalm 146 found me. It came as a challenge and as a gift. The psalm was speaking to me, for me, but also against me. It became a mirror and a guide for this journey of mine. With a bit of exaggeration it could be said that the psalm is a hermeneutical key that helps to discern the criteria for kingdom obedience today.

From that time on I have been speaking with and about the psalms many times. If you are familiar with my preaching you have the absolute right to be tired of it.

Then I was asked to speak about Psalm 146 at World Vision's International Council. This took place in Guatemala in September 1992. Since I had to speak in English—which I usually do not do in Brazil—I decided to write the text of my exposition down. That is the reason this book became a possibility. Thanks for the challenge!

Since I am a part of World Vision and I was talking to World Vision people, it was only natural that

I attempt to bring our mutual experience in community work and with the poor into dialogue with the text. I also want to see many Christians and their churches become involved with the poor and their communities.

Furthermore, I was also conscious—impossible to overlook in my exposition—that we were in Latin America and the year was 1992. The shadow of Christopher Columbus pervaded Latin America that year. The task of interpreting 500 years of colonization also included the challenge of interpreting 500 years of evangelization. In Latin America, the sword and the cross arrived together at the same beach.

Another consideration was that we were in Guatemala, where most of the population is of Indian descent with stories of discrimination to tell. Also, it is in Guatemala that the evangelical church has experienced the highest rate of growth in all Latin America. As we know, by growing the church becomes more visible and openly faces the unavoidable challenge of participating in national life.

Then there was Mary. She came into our picture

with beauty and strength. As we will see later, Mary's Magnificat is one of the most beautiful pieces of poetry in the Bible. Its similarity with Psalm 146 is tremendous. While I started by reading the psalm by itself, I ended up reading it alongside the Magnificat. I hope you will enjoy this experience as much as I did.

Psalm 146

Praise the Lord.

Praise the Lord, O my soul.
 I will praise the Lord all my life;
 I will sing praise to my God as long as I live.

Do not put your trust in princes,
 in mortal men, who cannot save.
When their spirit departs, they return to the ground;
 on that very day their plans come to nothing.

Blessed is he whose help is the God of Jacob,
 whose hope is in the Lord his God,
the Maker of heaven and earth,
 the sea, and everything in them—
 the Lord, who remains faithful forever.
He upholds the cause of the oppressed
 and gives food to the hungry.
The Lord sets prisoners free,
 the Lord gives sight to the blind,
the Lord lifts up those who are bowed down,
 the Lord loves the righteous.
The Lord watches over the alien
 and sustains the fatherless and the widow,
 but he frustrates the ways of the wicked.

The Lord reigns forever,
 your God, O Zion, for all generations.

Praise the Lord.

The Magnificat: Luke 1:46-55

My soul praises the Lord
    and my spirit rejoices in God my Savior,
    for he has been mindful of the humble state of his
        servant.
From now on all generations will call me blessed,
    for the Mighty One has done great things for me—
    holy is his name.
His mercy extends to those who fear him,
    from generation to generation.
He has performed mighty deeds with his arm;
    he has scattered those who are proud in their
        inmost thoughts.
He has brought down rulers from their thrones
    but has lifted up the humble.
He has filled the hungry with good things
    but has sent the rich away empty.
He has helped his servant Israel,
    remembering to be merciful
to Abraham and his descendants forever,
    even as he said to our fathers.

Sing praises to the Lord

Praise the Lord.
Praise the Lord, O my soul.
I will praise the Lord all my life;
I will sing praise to my God as long as I live.
(Psalm 146:1-2)

My soul praises the Lord . . .
for he has been mindful of
the humble state of his servant.
(Luke 1:46b, 48a)

Two pregnant women and a hug

IT ALL HAPPENED very quickly. How moving it was to see these two pregnant women hugging each other. Two pregnant women hugging each other makes a funny picture. Still, this was a different hug—it was transcendental.

The younger woman was still in the early stages of her pregnancy. Elizabeth, the older one, was well advanced in her pregnancy. This may explain why she just stood there, hands over her pregnant womb, a big smile on her face and her eyes somewhat hypnotized by the dancing-jumping-jumping-dancing picture of the younger woman. She looked like she was quietly struggling to hold back her emotions. The moment was loaded with a joyful electricity. With the happiness of this encounter almost visible in the air, the facial language of both women spoke about experiencing a very deep sense of fulfillment.

Still unable to calm down, the young woman—Mary was her name—anxiously searched for a way to express herself. Suddenly, a wonderful poem began to flow from her lips. While Mary recited her poem, everything around her fell into a deep silence. Even the two boys in the women's wombs, who just a few moments before had also tried to dance, became quiet and felt the significance of this moment and the beauty of this poem. Can we also listen as they listened?

My soul praises the Lord
and my spirit rejoices in God my Savior,
for he has been mindful of the humble state of
his servant.
From now on all generations will call me blessed . . .

The Magnificat, which emerged from Mary's lips because of the encounter between these two pregnant women, is one of the most beautiful and profound passages in the Bible. I think only a woman could have produced it. Only a feminine soul could capture the emotion and significance of the hour. Words, in this densely loaded and highly contagious context, had to be played out in poetry. Prose, discourses, cerebral statements were all too limited, dry and poor to express the melody and significance of that hour.

Since I am not a poet, I cannot evaluate Mary's poetry. Yet as a theologian I would say she impresses by the wealth and depth of what she says, and she is contagious because of how she says it. She has a deep sense of God's presence in history and of history's role in God's hands. She has a clear picture of what God is trying to do and how he is doing it. This is why joy and even surprise so overwhelmed her.

God's inclusion of her in the process of fulfilling his promise—the promise of bringing a new time, a messianic promise—continues to astonish her.

Mary is a poet and theologian who speaks out of a profound experience of being captured by and being captive to God's calling. The content of her poem is simultaneously amazing, profound and scary. It turns the usual order of things upside down: the choice of Mary herself is just one example of this.

The proud are dispersed, rulers lose their thrones and the rich leave with empty hands. This does not usually happen; it's a dream. The humble are lifted up, the hungry are filled with good things and Mary is miraculously pregnant. It all sounded impossible, and yet her pregnancy was very real. Just look at her! Mary, the pregnant theologian, knew that this pregnancy was a fact produced by God. It was God's way of writing his history—the history of salvation.

It is not in vain that E. Stanley Jones calls the Magnificat "the world's most revolutionary document." Throughout this book it will be a hermeneutical companion in our journey with and through

Psalm 146. These two passages are so similar, have so much in common, that I could not resist the temptation to let them walk hand in hand—to our enrichment, surprise and even provocation.

Listen to the tune and thunder of the psalm

The 146th Psalm is beautiful. It is my favorite psalm. I hope that by the end of this journey we are converted by it and to it, heart and mind.

This psalm has a long history of influencing the people of God. For example, it was a source of inspiration to well-known hymn writers in the history of Christian hymnology. Paul Gerhardt's famous *Du meine Seele singe, wohlauf und singe schön* ("Sing, thou my soul, arise and sing beautifully"), and Herrn-Schmidt's acclaimed *Lobe den Herren, o meine Seele*[1] ("Praise the Almighty, my soul"), are only two examples of this.

As for us, we want to join those forerunners in praising the Lord by borrowing the psalm's language and poetry to sing his praises as long as we live. Psalm 146, and many other psalms, is a continuous invitation to praise the Lord. As part of the fifth book of the Book of Psalms (Psalms 107-150),

Psalm 146 is part of a small group of five psalms (146-150) called *Hallel* because they start and conclude with *Hallelujah*, or "Praise the Lord."[2]

The liturgical richness of the psalms is immense. Psalm 146 itself was, according to Weiser, incorporated into the practice of daily morning prayers within the tradition of later Judaism.[3] The Christian church has long since discovered that the psalms are an enormous resource to inspire and guide the church in its worship life. In Latin America, for instance, it is interesting to see how much the psalms have inspired our hymnology during the past decades. We sing the psalms all over again in today's worship services.

Yet we need to do this with care. We must avoid the temptation to select only those portions of the psalms that fit easily into our particular tradition, or that are convenient to our own theological position, or that do not question our priorities and selective obedience. This is why we want to relate to all of Psalm 146, and we will do so step by step as we converse with the psalmist and with the Magnificat's author.

By summarizing "the message of the Psalms," John Goldingay suggests they underline four areas: praise, protest, telling what God has done, and proclaiming God's greatness.[4] I suggest that we will be well served by applying these emphases to Psalm 146. There is a note of each in the psalm, as we will see. If we can relate praise to protest, our journey in discipleship is underway and we will keep good company with the psalmist.

Unfortunately, much of our evangelical tradition is unable to incorporate the biblical protest theme within our own collective or personal Christian experiences. Such a theological understanding and ecclesial praxis has often taught us that once you become a Christian there will be easy answers for all questions.

As a result, we cannot dive into the depths and conflicts of a psalm such as this. We sing evangelical choruses and hope everything falls into place. Because of this, we avoid involvement in complex issues such as the search for justice and the search to end the circle of oppression, issues raised by the psalmist.

With such a theology we are far from the psalmist and Mary's Magnificat, impoverishing not only our liturgical life but our whole Christian experience as well. For in their words of praise to the Lord, readiness to serve, and a rereading of history in the light of God's promises, the denunciation of evil and injustice and the proclamation of God's victory over all forces of death go hand in hand. This is what Psalm 146 is all about. Are we willing and ready to make this our itinerary of faith?

Everything that has breath praise the Lord

The church in Latin America is young, lively, and visibly growing. If you had a little time to spend there, getting to know the life of its growing church, you would quickly conclude that praising the Lord is a very important element of the everyday life of the church. It would not be an exaggeration to speak of a *praise renewal* and a hymnological renewal occurring within many churches in Latin America.

This emphasis on praise has two components. One is cultural and forms a significant part of the so-called Pentecostal tradition. The Latin culture is a noisy culture, a street culture. People prefer to spend their time outside and not inside—when they have an "inside"—talking and not meditating, laughing or crying and not thinking, singing and not elaborating philosophical propositions. The Pentecostal tradition, more than any other Christian tradition, perceived this aspect of Latin culture and incorporated it into its liturgical experience.

Many who come from my tradition, that is, mainline Protestantism, may be a little disturbed if they go to a typical Pentecostal worship service. However, this may be a healthy experience. I would risk stating that most of the so-called historic Protestant churches are so directed by and tied to their past, with their roots "properly" established in the North, that they have lost the chance to develop a liturgical expression that establishes a healthy dialogue between a sound theological foundation and the cultural expression of the land where they worship God.

Another part of the recent worship tradition in Latin America goes by the name of the charismatic renewal. For the most part, this tradition finds its roots within the small Latin American middle class—reaching many professionals—and it builds upon the assumption that *big is beautiful.*

This tradition works toward gathering many people in worship meetings that are three to four hours long, where singing praises has a key, if not central, place. To stay on our feet for one to two hours singing the same choruses, clapping and raising our hands and practicing a few steps of liturgical dance, is more than most of our traditions allow or invite us to do. Yet these churches experience the highest rate of growth, and not only in Latin America. I would dare to say that if the psalmist were in Latin America, he would try to practice a few dance steps in response to a contagious melody that puts Latin American rhythm to an old poem:

> Praise the Lord.
> Praise the Lord, O my soul.
>> I will praise the Lord all my life;
>> I will sing praise to my God as long as I live.

Like Mary, the psalmist is a poet. Like Mary, he speaks with his heart and makes emotionally loaded statements that are difficult to measure on concrete levels. After all, what does it mean to commit oneself to "sing praises to my God as long as I live?" To try to measure the levels of continuity or discontinuity in the practice of praise, however, would mean to miss the point badly.

A poem reflects a moment, a commitment, and a posture. This is what the psalmist is trying to share with us. His experience of God's presence, his commitment to God's calling and his perception of God's action are deep, overwhelming and contagious. He finds that the best way to deal with and express his experience and conviction is to start to sing, and like Mary he sings praises to the Lord. Like Mary he gives his poem a sound and solid theological base: he sings about God's faithfulness to his promises, God's decisive and preferential action in history and God's final and undeniable victory:

> *The Lord reigns forever,*
>   *your God, O Zion, for all generations.*
> *Praise the Lord.*

What is there to sing about?

A serious temptation faced by the praise renewal movement in Latin America is that of becoming a superficial, alienating movement. The formal liturgical tradition faces the temptation of becoming mechanical and repetitive. The recent praise tradition, as expressed especially within the "communities movement," faces the temptation of becoming theologically shallow and contextually alienating, despite its cultural connections.

I would suggest that we test our life of praise in the light of Mary's Magnificat as well as in the light of the 146th Psalm. In both cases the poems are an expression of God's action and a hymn to God's faithfulness. As people of God, our praise to him "as long as we live" is not just a community feast but a proclamation and commitment as well. Let me explain what I mean.

1. *To praise the Lord is a communal act that should help to create and build community.*

Referring to the Psalms, John Goldingay says that "praising God in the Psalms is a corporate affair." He continues: "Whether it is praise, protest, thanksgiving or proclamation, it happens together."[5]

We should integrate this tradition with our praising experience. I fear that much of our praising activity runs the risk of representing a search for a personal emotional experience that helps me "feel good."

Many choruses and hymns that we sing repeatedly in our churches represent a spiritualized theology that is rich in heavenly language, eschatological expressions and easy promises of well-being.

These same hymns and choruses, however, are very poor in incarnational commitments, a sound reading of God's action in history and a good understanding of God's kingdom promises that we want to see fulfilled in the life of people and communities. As people of God we need to sing about what God has done in our lives and what he still wants to do in lives and through our lives. To praise the Lord is a community affair. It is a kingdom service.

2. *To praise the Lord is an act pregnant with missiological content. It is a proclamation of God's faithfulness and promises.*

To repeat God's faithfulness nourishes our lives, tells us that we are not alone, and announces to the world that he can be counted on. Proclaiming his promises says that history has a meaning, that life has worth and value, and that God is in control.

By announcing his promises we also make public God's intention of salvation for all. He is a God of life who is willing to give life, as shown in and through Jesus Christ. To praise the Lord means to announce and live out the good news that the God of life is offering life to all who carry in and with themselves the signs of death, who live in an environment of death.

In this sense, to praise the Lord is the privilege of a special people, a people on a journey. Our journey is of the kingdom and while we go on the way we celebrate—as long as we live—God's faithfulness to his people, and we invite everyone to become part of his people and his celebration. This message is worth celebrating in poetry. Mary and the psalmist have shown us the way.

3. *Excessive praise might be the problem of some Christian communities. It is certainly not my problem.*

It is not the problem of World Vision, the context in which these reflections were born. And I do not think it is the problem of most of those who are reading this book.

We are too pragmatic and conflictive for that. Our pragmatism makes us too results-oriented to have the time and even patience to get together with those who, without a guilt complex, spend time raising their hands to heaven in praise. By being too conflictive I mean that we have seen and been in touch with too much misery, suffering and injustice—that is why we cannot just raise our hands in "naïve" adoration.

How many of us have experienced the inability to sing praise with our well-dressed congregations on Sunday morning because the images of the week are still with us: a dying child, a broken family, a community without a drop of water, an entire Indian community decimated by military troops? We feel like crying, not singing.

Those among us who are unwilling to live out their faith disconnected from the death and suffering that surround us face the challenge of singing a song of hope in the midst of violence. This song is a song that announces God's promises to the poor and the little ones. It is a song that denounces the evil one and those who are at his service. This is why we are invited to put a melody to the psalmist's poem:

> The Lord watches over the alien
> and sustains the fatherless and the widow,
> but he frustrates the ways of the wicked.

We do not need to close our eyes while singing praises to the Lord. We can sing praises with our eyes open, willing to see and feel the pain of the world—and then our eyes will meet God's eyes. We do not need to hide ourselves in well-protected buildings to praise the Lord. On the contrary, the world has to hear our praise to perceive that there is a God who wants to enter people's lives and change their histories by marking them with peace, justice and joy—his marks.

We do not need to refine our praise beautifully and search for the best acoustic environment for our praise to be well received by God. He invites us to praise him while following the steps of Jesus in the dirty streets of the Galilee of yesterday and today.

This is why God invites us to praise him even in

the midst of challenge and pain, yet also surrounded by his faithfulness and promises. Let us put melodies into God's stories so that people may believe. Let us not forget that we are in good company. Mary is inviting us to sing with her:

> *My soul praises the Lord*
> *and my spirit rejoices in God my Savior,*
> *for he has been mindful of the humble state of*
> *his servant.*

Notes

1. Arthur Weiser, *Die Psalmen*, ATD 14/15 (Vandenhoeck & Ruprecht: Göttingen, 1966), p. 573.

2. Derek Kidner, *Salmos 73-150: Introdução e Comentário* (Vida Nova and Mundo Cristão: São Paulo, 1981). p. 400. Most contemporary authors divide the book of Psalms into five major groups, starting, respectively, with Psalms 1, 42, 73, 90, and 107. Each of those psalm series concludes with a doxology. See Kidner, *Salmos 1-72: Introdução e Comentário* (Vida Nova and Mundo Cristão: São Paulo, 1980), p. 15.

3. Weiser, p. 574.

4. John Goldingay, "The Message of Psalms," in *The Message of the Bible* (Lion Book: Tring/England, Batavia/USA, Sydney/Australia, 1988), pp. 76-77.

5. Goldingay, p. 77.

Keep your feet on the ground!

Do not put your trust in princes,
in mortal men, who cannot save.
When their spirit departs, they return to the ground;
on that very day their plans come to nothing.
(Psalm 146:3-4)

. . . he has scattered those
who are proud in their inmost thoughts.
He has brought down rulers from their thrones . . .
(Luke 1:51b-52a)

What to say in 1992?

THE INTERPRETATIONS about the significance of the
year 1992 were, in Latin America, abundant and
conflicting. Reminders were everywhere that 500
years ago, European colonizers reached our shores
and brought with them their swords, their appetite

for gold, their church, and their faith. These things came simultaneously.

That is why when we speak about the history of evangelization in Latin America, we also speak about the history of a continent that the oppressive forces of Spain and Portugal conquered violently. In conquering our land, these countries were also officially commissioned to represent the interests of the church in that same land.

In fact, we find ourselves in a kind of historical trap. Do we celebrate or do we lament? Do we express gratitude for the arrival of the gospel on our shores or do we protest against a type of evangelization that allowed itself to become an instrument of domestication, oppression and death to thousands of native inhabitants, their cultures, languages and customs? Frankly, it is difficult to decide how best to speak of these things. There is so much ambiguity in this history of evangelization.

But we should not forget that much of the history of Christian mission has this mark of ambiguity. Also, we should recognize that the type of Christianity that came to Latin America was Constantinian. This model pervades much of the historical practice of Christian mission that Christendom was and is—sometimes to a greater or lesser extent—inwardly contaminated by a disturbing alliance between church and state, cross and sword, conversion and coercion, power and servility.

A healthy suspicion

In Latin America in recent decades, some Christian forces have been saying that we should be suspicious about the kind of Christianity that needs the state to insure its place in society, that needs to apply mechanisms of coercion to get its message through, that needs "official permission" to exist.

Those same forces emphasized the need to rediscuss the impact of the dynamics of the Christian faith on society. Such an impact should not follow the dynamics of institutional and hierarchical power, and of association with the established political power. Instead, it should break forth from the grassroots because of community involvement and the convocational and transforming strength of the gospel message itself.

It should have a decisive impact on society, be it

in terms of proclamation or denunciation. Of denunciation, because the Christian faith cannot accept what can be called the mechanisms of death that have destroyed so many lives and communities throughout the centuries. Violence, exploitation, oppression, injustice, hunger, nakedness—these are signs of death that are the sad and morbid daily bread in so many places all over, but not only in, Latin America. Of proclamation, because the gospel of Jesus Christ is a message of life that promotes life, and it struggles for life in the midst of the abundant signs of death. Life is possible because Jesus is life and in his name life comes alive.

In recent years, Liberation Theology called this critical way of relating to historical processes, to ideologies, to political, economic and religious systems a "hermeneutic of suspicion." This hermeneutic recognizes the need to think critically, to interpret reality, and to unmask the distortions and mechanisms of oppression under which so many people live today. It also means to unmask a false conscience and a tendency to support uncritically the status quo with all its inequities.

I recommend it as a useful category, even if it is not neutral, as it cannot be. If Christians and Christian communities had been less naïve and more suspicious in their relationships with systems, ideological packages and messianic proposals throughout history, we could have avoided much suffering. The psalmist tells us something about it:

> *Do not put your trust in princes,*
> *in mortal men, who cannot save.*
> *When their spirit departs, they return to the ground;*
> *on that very day their plans come to nothing.*

The psalmist says "No!"

In chapter one we rejoiced with the psalmist, with Mary, and with the people of God about God's glory, his insertion into history and his faithfulness. The psalmist, so to speak, said "Yes." He said yes to God himself, and yes to our directing the whole of our lives to God's glory. "I will sing praise to my God as long as I live," said the psalmist—and all the people said, "Amen."

Now the psalmist says "No!" He says no to princedoms, ideological packages, dictatorial systems, and to scientific myths of finality, as well as to arrogant episcopacies, their religious boxes and impressive cathedrals. "Do not put your trust in princes, in mortal men," he warns us.

When to say yes and when to say no is not always easy to discern. As we saw earlier, when talking about 500 years of the history of evangelization in Latin America, the church very often got lost between the yes and the no. Some political systems and religious packages should have received our resounding and unequivocal no, but instead got a "Let it pass" or even a yes. At other times, when a clear yes was needed, silence came as a response, or a no was pronounced.

Elements of our native cultures, as met by Spanish and Portuguese invaders, deserved affirmation and not destruction. The church should have assured the right of the native people to keep their land and make their decisions regarding religion freely. But the yes never really came, and millions of the native inhabitants lost their land, their right to make decisions, and even their lives.

By saying no to "princes . . . who cannot save," the psalmist is saying three different things: 1) he is breaking down all the "walls and curtains" that were built up and that have separated people or nations throughout history; 2) he is making a profound statement about how God sees all people as equal in his eyes and how this should be true for us as well; and 3) he is pointing in a direction that makes it possible for us to follow the way of trust and not the one of suspicion.

Let us look a little more deeply into this.

Walls, curtains, and the conflict of finitude

If you ever go to the Philippines, do not miss the opportunity to visit Malacañang ("Here lives a nobleman") Palace. Malacañang Palace was the official residence of the presidents of the Philippines and thus it was the home of the former dictator Ferdinand Marcos and his wife Imelda.

Just to remind you, Imelda Marcos was the woman who became famous because of her thousands of pairs of shoes. Ferdinand Marcos was the man who lost the presidential elections in 1986, did not want to admit his defeat and tried to hold on to power as long as possible. He eventually had to flee, and the palace became a museum, a theater for public mockery and irony.

Two very different "Ferdinand Marcoses," so to speak, used to live in the palace: the dreamed-about one and the real one. Big, colorful portraits on the walls displayed the dreamed-about one. In those pictures Marcos was young, strong and handsome: the man every woman wanted, the hunter every lion was afraid of, the invincible fighter unable to find a challenger, the president each Filipino dreamed about.

The real Marcos was very different. He was afraid, old and sick. All the palace windows that faced the street were shut for security reasons. The oxygen tube and the mini-hospital close to Marcos' room showed the vulnerability of a sick man. There was no way back, in spite of the portraits on the wall and the tanks in the streets.

Malacañang Palace can be seen as a recent version of the Tower of Babel, spoken about in Genesis 11. At the beginning of the day there is a sense of infinitude and the people's goal of making themselves eternal, struggling against their finitude and deciding, according to Genesis 11:4, "Come, let us build ourselves a city, with a tower that reaches to the heavens, so that we may make a name for ourselves . . ." At the end of the day, confusion, vulnerability and a sense of emptiness remain: "When their spirit departs, they return to the ground; on that very day their plans come to nothing" says the psalmist.

In other words, be careful with your well-kept illusions—about yourself, your beautiful image in the mirror, your political proposals, your economic resources, your scientific research, your highly computerized instruments or your church structures. They may all serve a purpose but it is a relative and limited one.

Therefore, do not try to eternalize your illusions—they are not worth living for. In fact, at the very moment you try to eternalize them, they will run like sand through your fingers. There you will stand with empty hands: "on that very day their plans come to nothing."

The democratic roots of the Christian faith

By saying "no" to absolute leaders, closed systems and arrogant ideologies, the psalmist also makes a beautiful statement about equality in the human community. So we are back to creation and to affirming God's creation, which states that all people are equal and that God is sovereign.

In God's creation there should be no room for attempts to establish qualitative differences between human beings because of culture, language, social scale, race or gender. We are all equal and equally created by God. As a collective mandate, we received the task and the privilege of responsibly administering life and resources. God is very democratic in the way he creates and maintains the human race and we should adopt that democratic pattern when exercising our stewardship mandate.

There are differences between persons, peoples and cultures, but these differences are not qualitative. These differences do not give any person or group the right to exercise dominion over or generate dependency in any other person, people or culture.

On the contrary, we can and should celebrate our differences as an expression of God's creativity and of human inventiveness in response to the challenge of collectively administering life in society. In addition, diversity can be understood on a complementary basis. We complement each other in and through our differences. In God's creation there is room for everyone. We need each other. In the human community there is room for a healthy dependency.

By stressing equality as a distinctive mark of God's creation I am not asking for a naïve egalitarianism that characterizes itself by mediocrity, paralysis and inefficiency. Nor am I standing up for an anarchic collectivism that has no room for social organization, political systems or economic structures. Each of these dimensions has a welcome place since each is at the service of people's well-being and survival.

When our human structures and differences are at the service of people's well-being and survival, they fulfill their functions. This is also the reason why they should neither create or maintain differences of a social or economic nature that the Creator himself did not intend. From the perspective of the Christian faith, the differences and systems that do not serve and help human beings and the human community live their lives as God intended are called sin and are expressions of brokenness.

The Christian faith always faces the challenge of finding the balance between utopia and reality, dream and nightmare. It feeds its dream by searching the heart of God and by always asking for God's intentionality. To live out God's intentionality also means to find fulfillment and human realization, and to find one's place in the human community. These dimensions of life, whether at the vertical or at the horizontal level, are inseparably interconnected. A rupture at one level will automatically reflect at the other level.

The Christian faith also works with a realistic concept of life. It is the reality of sin and its consequences that provides us with the tools of realism, helping us to avoid feeding dreams that have no historical and anthropological connections. This reality also helps us avoid building utopias that will only experience the pain of deliverance without giving birth or, in another image, will give birth to the wind without the materialization of a new hope.

The psalmist is aware of this. He knows what real life is about. This is probably why he introduces the concept of suspicion as a way of living and recommends the necessity of being aware of the reality of sin and of human finitude. After all, everything around us carries the mark of both.

The psalmist also says we should never forget that, in spite of the appearance of the infinitude of beauty and youth, of the splendor of princes and palaces, of the authoritarian cry of dictators, of the well-articulated discourse of political leaders, of the permanence of cathedrals, and of the apparent strength of institutions, they all remain under the risk of abandonment by the spirit and under the certainty that they will return to the ground.

People of faith drink water at another fountain

The psalmist is not finished. The ground does not have the last word. If this were not so, the psalmist will have left us with empty hands, in the midst of a nihilist anarchism that is a poor substitute for false hopes, idolatries and illusions.

The main reason the psalmist takes us through the difficult journey of recognizing our finitude and of adopting the criteria of suspicion is because he knows the way that takes us beyond the ground. It is faith in God that takes us beyond the ground and allows us to walk into the future with hope.

After taking us through a difficult No, the psalmist wants to help us visualize a solid YES. He wants our eyes to find that God has shown him-self, throughout history, to be faithful. This is a God who, in Mary's language, acts today according to what "he said to our fathers." But we will leave that for the next chapter.

The psalmist invites us into a fresh experience of praise and adoration. Only those who are willing to praise God with the same depth and freedom as the psalmist are invited by him to take the next step and to relativize princes and their palaces, ideologues and their advocates, systems and their executioners, economists and their packages, cathedrals and their bishops.

The psalmist invites us to redirect our eyes to the cross of Jesus, because this is the route that takes us beyond the ground. On this route we will meet Mary and the Samaritan woman, and it will

take us to a "spring of water welling up to eternal
life" (John 4:14).

God's name is faithfulness

Blessed is he whose help is the God of Jacob,
whose hope is in the Lord his God,
the Maker of heaven and earth,
the sea, and everything in them—
the Lord, who remains faithful forever.
(Psalm 146:5-6)

He has helped his servant Israel,
remembering to be merciful
to Abraham and his descendants forever,
even as he said to our fathers.
(Luke 1:54-55)

The image issue

EVERYONE IN our so-called Christian society carries around a few images of God. If you say you don't, I will not believe you.

I am not saying that you are carrying handmade images of God with you. I am talking about the images of God that are in your mind. Some of these images are old because they come from your childhood.

Perhaps you were afraid to walk to your room in the dark, and your father told you not to fear because the good heavenly Father would be waiting for you in your room: "He is good at seeing in the dark." So you walk into your room imagining this heavenly Father with a mixture of special eyes and glasses that allow him to see in the dark and protect you from danger.

To have many images about who God is is almost a type of Christian folklore. In our collective imagery, God comes to our imagination sometimes as a protector, sometimes as a punisher, as an elder brother or one who disciplines a disobedient child, a firefighter ready to extinguish fires in our life, or as a healer to bind up our wounds. To have cultivated different images of God is part of the Western Christian culture in which many of us grew up.

I must have been fifteen years old. I was working during the day and studying at night. A raffle was being held at my workplace. I bought a ticket. I wanted the prize very badly. I do not even remember what it was, but I do remember that I wanted to give it to my mother as a gift.

Since I knew I was not one of those persons who have a calling to win prizes, I decided to pray. God the omnipotent could enable me to win that prize. After all, wasn't he omnipotent? Why could he not do that for me? I even started to bargain with God. Besides my noble intention of giving the prize to my mother, I would "amend" my life in many areas. I enumerated these areas in my heartfelt and pleading prayer. But I did not win the prize. What a disappointment! What kind of God is God anyway?

How to understand God and how to relate to him is an old problem, and one that is not restricted to images or frustrations from adolescence. It is part of our adult life and part of our collective experience. It is within our churches and in the worlds of science and philosophy, with their attempts to find, define, and understand God.

Do you remember the Soviet astronaut who

announced from space that God did not exist because the astronaut did not find God up there? It is also interesting to go to the history of philosophy and start to enumerate the different attempts to define or describe God. God is the "great maker of the universe," the "summum bonum," the "invisible force," and so on.

A problem with these images, concepts and definitions of God is that if we could conceptualize him he would no longer be God. He would become a slave-God, imprisoned by our definitions and articulations. When captured by our definitions and expressed in philosophical categories, God becomes small, abstract and distant. We are all very much caught up in the old Greek tradition with its philosophical dreams, avoiding the incarnated Judaic categories where God puts his feet on the ground and becomes immersed in history.

As Christians whose understanding of the Christian faith is very much mediated by Western and philosophical categories, we have difficulties perceiving God in terms of relationships and not concepts; immersion, not distance; and historical action, not abstract statements. Very often God becomes our point of reference, but not someone who is very close to us. We understand that our lives are in God's hands, but those hands are big, strong, masculine and distant. They are not fit for hugging, or caressing or guiding us.

Furthermore, God is our Father, but our souls and our future—that is, eternal life—are his primary concern. He is good and merciful, but the church receives most of his attention and he gives priority to church people. He is great but he is active especially in communities and countries where Christians are the majority.

God is present in ways beyond our imagination!

How to understand and perceive God's global, loving and transforming presence and action in history has been a very important issue in Latin American theology in recent decades. A child is dying, a mother does not have any food to put on the table, a husband lost his job, a community's harvest was burned by terrorists or by the military, a democratic government was overthrown, a revolution took place—where is God in all this?

In our theological journey with these and many other questions, we joyfully rediscover and are surprised by how very close God is to us—his name is Jesus, the Nazarene. In addition, by rereading the Gospels and experiencing anew the call to discipleship, we rediscover a theological principle called incarnation.

This journey of ours is not necessarily a new one. Christians have always known that to know God we must meet Jesus. We also know that Jesus became flesh to provide salvation for humankind. Yet somehow, and in a broader sense, this "dogmatic knowledge" was difficult for Latin Americans to relate to Latin America and to our situation of poverty, exploitation and despair. Again, it looked as if God's main concern was with the soul and not with material things like bread and water, with the future more than the present, with a person more than the community, with the church more than society.

In theological terms, it looked as if God's main interest was in the expiatory dimension of Jesus' cross and with articulating a "theology of glory" concerning the resurrection of Jesus. Then we read the Gospels again and so many ideas struck us, ideas that to us had the taste of fresh water after a long journey on a hot summer day.

a) We rediscovered the centrality of the message of the kingdom of God as lived out and announced by Jesus, and the immediate consequences of it in history.

b) We became aware in a new way that, in his time, Jesus' ministry meant liberation to many children and women, blind, crippled, sick and oppressed people.

c) We recognized that Jesus intentionally decided to spend most of his ministry in the culturally and ethnically mixed, and socially and economically poor area of Galilee, instead of in Jerusalem, the center of religious and secular power.

d) We saw the clear and repeated pattern of behavior by Jesus' enemies, who so feared that Jesus would break down their well-established monopoly of interpreting God's Word to the people that they decided to get rid of him.

e) We came to understand that the crucifixion was an obvious political consequence of Jesus' religious, cultural and sociopolitical options, and not just God's act of mercy of giving his Son to die for all humankind.

f) In a new way, we saw the resurrection of Jesus as a seed of hope which can and needs to become a seed of transformation in the fertile yet arid soil of old and contemporary Galilees. Jesus is alive! Rejoice, all the children of the world!

We placed every one of the above aspects in a theological practice that focused on the centrality of the kingdom of God and identified the principle of incarnation as a fundamental pillar in a solid New Testament theology. Within this context God became a partner in a suffering world and the source of hope to all those who could not look beyond despair without him.

In addition, the way in which God relates to us, to the world—through the incarnation of Jesus—should be the pattern that the church uses in relation to the world, in its mission. So much for theology. And don't worry—I did not forget Psalm 146. On the contrary.

The God of Jacob is a God of history

Smile! The psalmist says "yes" again. He points out the way to go, a way to live. He shares a secret:

> *Blessed is he whose help is the God of Jacob,*
> *whose hope is in the Lord his God,*
> *the Maker of heaven and earth,*
> *the sea, and everything in them—*
> *the Lord, who remains faithful forever.*

Who does not want to be blessed? Who does not want to be happy, to make good decisions, and to walk on solid ground? Real life, however, does not seem to go this way for very many people. Why? Jesus revealed a secret accepted by few: "For whoever wants to save his life will lose it, but whoever loses his life for me and for the gospel will save it" (Mark 8:35).

The psalmist, in his way, told us to be suspicious of answers that do not have the flavor of the eternal but only the smell of the earth and the destiny of returning to "the ground."

But this was not his last word. He has more to

say. He points his finger and redirects our eyes to history, where we can see the many clear steps of God's presence and actions. Steps of care, steps of faithfulness, steps of direction, steps of hope. Look at history, says the psalmist. Watch the lives of so many who have found a light to follow, a secret to share, the way to go:

> *Blessed is he whose help is the God of Jacob,*
> *whose hope is in the Lord his God . . .*

Do you remember Jacob? Ours is the God of Jacob. Our God is the God of history. We can verify his decisive action and firm steps in history. He is the God of Abraham and Sarah, Jacob and Rachel, Moses and Miriam, Deborah and Simeon, Peter and Mary, Paul and Lydia, Aquila and Priscilla, Luther and Katherine; he is our God. Follow the steps of his action in history and his care, his faithfulness, and his guidance will conquer you.

We might be like Jacob, with many dubious events to stain our biography, but even so God will not abandon us. We might be like Abraham, with events in our lives that we do not like to remember, but even so God keeps his promises. The secret does not rely on a record of good behavior by Jacob or Abraham. God's faithfulness is the secret the psalmist wants to share with us. The psalmist insists on presenting to us the one source of help and hope he knows: the Lord God, the God of Jacob.

History is not a product of fortune. Nor is it a prisoner of evil and despair. History is in God's hands. While there is such a thing as history, while people are alive on earth, God will keep his distinctive note: caring for Jacob, fulfilling his promise through Sarah, choosing Mary as the mother of Jesus, acting through the open house of Priscilla and Aquila, proclaiming his word through Luther, and renewing the hope of survival for many who, by following the steps of Jacob, will witness God's faithfulness.

Our God is not a tribal God

While our God makes himself known in history, it does not imprison him. While our God is the God of Jacob, a personal God, those who follow him cannot encapsulate him. While we can see God's acts in our midst, he can never be limited by or to us. He is not a tribal God. He cannot be limited by or to any culture or language, nation or system.

Look around, says the psalmist, see the sky, feel the warmth of the earth, breathe in the freshness of the sea. God is the Creator, "the maker of heaven and earth, the sea, and everything in them." He is God universal.

This statement is a delight. It breaks down the limits of the horizon and takes us to encounter a God who is impossible to describe, to understand or to define. Let's just jump into his arms, rejoice, and follow him!

Yet there will always be a place in his arms for someone else. Then let us try not to limit God to our experience, doctrine, denomination or culture. God himself breaks down all limits, to be found by all as helper, companion, source of hope, and redeemer. He is the source of life.

Bringing history and nature together

The psalmist has put together a masterpiece of theology. History and nature are no longer realities apart. The Creator, the Lord of history, and Jacob's personal God all belong together. Every dimension of life belongs to God and experiences his care. To Jacob he is faithful, he keeps leaving his marks in history, and all creation continuously experiences his care.

If we look at our Christian tradition we will easily see how difficult it is to keep these dimensions of God and of our relationship with him in a holistic perspective. Time after time we try to separate what God wants to keep whole. If we stress God as Creator, we risk keeping him at a distance or retiring him after "finishing his work." If we stress the historicity of God's action, the temptation emerges to keep him so busy with complex historical developments that a personal relationship with him seems out of the picture.

The psalmist is telling us that God the Creator is not only faithful to his creation in general, but to every creature in particular. He wants to establish a personal relationship with each of his human creatures. He does not merely create the world and then distance himself from it. He maintains his creation and has a primary and continuing interest in its administration and the development of history.

The Christian faith is a beautiful faith: the origin of the world, the historical development of creation, the divine value of each human being, and the establishment of living relations with each other and with God himself are all dimensions of the God who is whole in himself and faithful to his creation and his intention of salvation. He "remains faithful forever," (Ps. 146:6) proclaims the psalmist.

The task of collectively administering creation, with its resources and possibilities, is a mandate given by God to all people in every generation. Understanding this mandate means Christians should be pioneers in the effort to keep the earth alive.

What we see very often, however, is that other groups claim more responsibility for this issue than many Christians and their churches do. The reason for this is that we are captive to a modernist assumption that we probably already theoretically reject. We accept the division between the spiritual and the material and we spiritualize the Christian faith itself. We embrace a materialist concept and belief in progress that assumes that natural resources are here to fulfill our "increasing needs" and are a source of profit.

The psalmist has a strong word for us: Take the consequences of your creation doctrine more seriously. Join forces with those who are fighting to preserve nature—"heaven, earth, and sea"—which is God's creation. We are stewards of these things.

Who is God? What is he doing?

He upholds the cause of the oppressed
and gives food to the hungry.
The Lord sets prisoners free,
the Lord gives sight to the blind,
the Lord lifts up those who are bowed down,
the Lord loves the righteous.
The Lord watches over the alien
and sustains the fatherless and the widow,
but he frustrates the ways of the wicked.
(Psalm 146:7-9)

He has performed mighty deeds with his arm;
he has scattered those
who are proud in their inmost thoughts.
He has brought down rulers from their thrones
but has lifted up the humble.
He has filled the hungry with good things
but has sent the rich away empty.
(Luke 1:51-53).

Parul Das' story

IN THE PREVIOUS CHAPTER we already talked a lot about who God is. There we saw that faithfulness in relationships, identification through incarnation and closeness to his human creation are distinctive marks of God himself. Now it is time to go a step further and to ask more specifically where God is and whom he takes time with.

To start let me share with you a small piece of the life of Parul Das, a 15-year-old girl from Bangladesh. It all happened during a big flood in that country. Listen with your heart, please:

> When the water came in, my father sent us to a shelter. He stayed behind to protect our belongings. My mother carried my 4-year-old brother, and I carried my 11-year-old sister. It was dark and raining. The water came up to our shoulders. There was thunder and lightning. Pieces of houses and tree branches rushed by and scratched us. My sister was crying and shivering, but I could not comfort her. The wind was too loud for talking.
>
> I heard my grandmother cry out as she was swept away, but I could not help her. A big wave came and knocked me off the road. I heard my mother calling in the darkness. I cried, "Come this way." Probably she answered, but I didn't hear her.

A half hour later I reached the shelter. The roof was so crowded I thought it would collapse. The wind burned our skin and the rain made us shiver. My sister was crying. I said, "Don't worry. Mommy is somewhere and after the rain we will meet again."

In the morning I saw my mother walking on the road. Our brother was still in her arms, but he was dead. He drowned while we were walking. My mother spent the night holding him in a thorn tree. Later we found my grandmother's body. I cannot explain what terrible things happened that night, or why I did not die. If the same thing should happen again, I don't think I would have the courage to survive.[1]

Is there anything that we could possibly say? Maybe the only possible response is silence, letting the tears roll down our own faces as we cry with Parul Das. She is only one of the many who are trying so hard not to give up "the courage to survive."

The touch of Jesus

Not long ago in Ecuador, I had to go and preach at the funeral of Deborah, the baby daughter of a good friend of mine. At that time of the year, it almost never rains in Ecuador, but at the precise hour of the funeral, it did rain. There I was, in the rain, crying and trying to say something that would come from the heart of God to our hearts, to the hearts of my friend, his wife and their daughters. Just as we are, I said, God is crying because little Deborah is dead. To my friend the rain became the tears of God shed over the death of Deborah. I don't think God got angry because of this interpretation. The same Jesus who wept (John 11:35) over the death of his friend Lazarus was with us that afternoon in Ecuador.

A most impressive and sensitive dimension of the gospel is what we could call the *touch of Jesus*. He put his arms around the children who felt rejected by the disciples. He stopped by the tree where Zacchaeus was and made it clear that he wanted to spend some time with Zacchaeus. He listened to the desperate cry of the blind man sitting by the roadside at Jericho. He was sensitive to the desperate plea of a father for his daughter: "Please come and put your hands on her so that she will be healed and live" (Mark 5:23). He ran the risk of absolving an adulterous woman: "Go now and leave your life of sin" (John 8:11).

In the streets and corners of Galilee where Jesus

spent most of his time of ministry, his presence became to many people both the possibility of having a shoulder to cry on and the challenge of looking beyond despair and finding the "courage to survive."

Therefore, to those who cry, in the rainy season or in the dry season, during childhood or in later days, in situations of loss and pain, in Bangladesh, São Paulo or Los Angeles, all are welcome to cry at the feet of Jesus. He will cry with them—a cry of pain, a cry of understanding, a cry of compassion, a cry that calls forth a new morning.

Parul, you should know that Jesus wants to walk with you when the next rain comes, to give you the courage to survive. He even wants to give you the courage to stretch out your hand to help your little neighbor, the one who is so afraid and struggling hard not to let go. Look around and you will find many who, in the name of Jesus, have found the light of a new day after a difficult night of rain and thunder. The psalmist knows about it.

> *He upholds the cause of the oppressed*
> *and gives food to the hungry.*

The Lord sets prisoners free,
    the Lord gives sight to the blind,
the Lord lifts up those who are bowed down,
    the Lord loves the righteous.
The Lord watches over the alien
    and sustains the fatherless and the widow...

The psalmist, Mary and Jesus know each other very well

We mentioned earlier what we called a theology of incarnation. We learned that God is not an abstract concept, a well elaborated idea, a distant judge or a tired father. He is here, he is close, he has become one of us in and through Jesus Christ. Through Jesus Christ we discover not only who God is but also where he is and who he enjoys being with.

Through Jesus Christ, God's priorities become clear. Jesus lived out God's priorities in the streets of Galilee. Also, the presence of Jesus, in acts and words, represented God's simultaneous "yes" and "no"—the possibility of life and the announcement of God's judgment. It all depends on how people position themselves before him and what they represent. The Gospels are full of examples that go in both directions. The psalmist himself at another time had worked on that same proposition: God cares for the poor, the weary and the oppressed, but the days of the wicked are numbered.

By going through our psalm again, looking carefully at verses seven to nine, we are forced to walk over ground that is very fertile, in terms of challenge and of risky interpretations. It is a walk between excitement and fear. Excitement, because these three verses are pregnant with hope. Fear, because these same verses turn the values and patterns of the world upside down.

It looks as though Mary is an expert in this. God lifts up the humble, like Mary, while he scatters the proud and the rulers lose their thrones. The hungry are fed, while the rich leave with empty hands.

If we read the psalm with one eye, so to speak, and the recent history of our evangelical theology in the West with the other eye, our conclusions will be dramatic. It's puzzling, for example, to discover how much time and energy we devoted to the impossible task of trying to show that God's priorities are for souls and individuals.

We worked hard to convince ourselves that what God prefers most is to see us preaching the gospel in a language that is linear and verbal, and singing Christian songs from the good old days. Also, we were taught to believe that if we do not sing these songs we are becoming modernists; if we do not preach the gospel in this narrow way we run the risk of becoming liberals; if we do not clearly show our commitment to saving souls, instead of helping the poor, we would be contaminated by the virus of what was known as the Social Gospel, and in more recent days, Liberation Theology.

All this might sound like the agenda of the sixties and seventies, but it might be that the sixties are still with us in more places and minds than we would like to believe.

I must confess that I would prefer not to enter this old discussion concerning the place of evangelism and social responsibility within the framework of the mission of the church. But the psalmist does not allow me to withdraw. He insists on asking, Where is God? What is he doing? Going a step further, the psalmist asks some more questions: Where am I? Where are you? Where is our church? What are we doing? In this context, this becomes the central question of discipleship.

By struggling our way through these questions we will find out that God is present among those whom we would often prefer to avoid. God is also doing what we would prefer not to be involved in—upholding the cause of the oppressed, giving food to the hungry, setting prisoners free, giving sight to the blind, lifting up those who are bowed down, loving the righteous, watching over the alien, sustaining the fatherless and the widow and frustrating the ways of the wicked. This is a scary and very difficult agenda.

Sometimes, when facing a difficult situation, I start making jokes or become ironic. It's an attempt to dilute the tension, to find a way out of the situation. Now our temptation could be to bargain with the psalmist and offer him an agreement. It could come out as a sort of world-charismatic-vision agreement. The charismatic folk would take care of the miraculous part, like giving sight to the blind. Christian development agencies would take care of another and even broader section. They would set up feeding centers for the hungry, provide health care and educational assistance for the orphans, stress micro-enterprises for the aliens and refugees, and teach widows to get involved in handicrafts and even encourage them to form a cooperative.

Together, the charismatics and the development agencies could set up two other programs. One of them would be a prison ministry and the other a counseling one, for people who are "bowed down."

As he reviews this offer of ours, with all its programs and activities, the psalmist may appear very happy. After all, he should be glad to see a serious Christian involvement in the areas of society where people struggle so hard not to give up their "courage to survive." In fact, many different segments of the evangelical church have been involved in a broad range of activities that include social service and assistance, and emotional and pastoral care to the little ones, to the poor and disfavored ones.

The psalmist, however, is not completely satisfied yet. There are still two words in the Psalm that he insists on calling our attention to: "oppressed" and "wicked." Silence! Frustrating silence! After all, you cannot do everything. We do have a limited calling. We cannot jeopardize the whole ministry because of a wrong emphasis. Maybe those two words are not really that important. They might even show up only accidentally in the Word. Isn't it possible that the psalmist is insisting on a secondary issue?

By raising these questions—this we must recognize—we still cannot look the psalmist in the eyes. When we finally look at him, we quickly conclude that our attempt to escape fell short. What is more, the psalmist is not an isolated voice. On the contrary, he is in good company, with the content of his psalm. He will patiently take us to the future, to listen to a voice that carries in itself the melody of a messianic promise. Listen to Mary:

> *He has performed mighty deeds with his arm;*
> *he has scattered those who are proud in their*
> *inmost thoughts.*
> *He has brought down rulers from their thrones*
> *but has lifted up the humble.*
> *He has filled the hungry with good things*
> *but has sent the rich away empty.*

There is a book called *The Upside-Down Kingdom*. I'm sure Mary did not read it, but she certainly drank from the same fountain. What Mary is saying, as we have already seen, is so strange, so different, so threatening, but also so refreshing and hopeful. It goes against everything we know and experience in our society—a competitive society—and, very often, in our churches.

To scatter the proud, to bring down rulers and to send the rich away empty means to subvert the order, to threaten the status quo, to break down the system. As we know, in the system we call the proud knowledgeable, the rulers keep power tightly in their hands and make sure things stay as they are, and the rich represent the buying power without which the consumer circle cannot operate.

However, Mary is not a sophisticated woman and she does not know anything about social analysis, hermeneutic keys for interpreting reality, and ideological presuppositions. She does not even miss these things.

But she is a powerful woman with a powerful message. Through her Magnificat, she becomes a precursor of the kingdom of God, as proclaimed and lived out by Jesus. And it is this message of the kingdom that turns everything around, to become a message of hope, especially to the poor, the humble and the oppressed.

Mary's choice to become the mother of the Messiah is a clear demonstration of how this illogical logic of the kingdom works. After all, Mary did not live in Jerusalem, but in Nazareth. She was not the daughter of the high priest, but only a Galilean woman who offered to God her most precious treasure: the gift of motherhood. It is within the strange and surprising logic of the kingdom that the angel finds Mary. It is only according to the values of the kingdom that the humble are recognized and promoted, and the hungry are filled with good things. Donald B. Kraybill, the author of the book I mentioned earlier called *The Upside-Down Kingdom*, expresses it this way:

> Mary expects the advent of the kingdom heralded by the Messiah to drastically upset the patterns of social structure. As a poor Galilean peasant girl, Mary anticipated the messianic reign to turn her social world upside down. The rich,

mighty, and proud in Jerusalem would be sent away. The poor of the earth around Galilee would be exalted and honored. Her longing and hope provides us with a key which fits the lock holding the secrets of the Upside-Down Kingdom.[2]

The kingdom of God represents a reality of hope precisely because it embraces the lonely, comforts the despairing, takes care of the abandoned, protects the exploited, liberates the oppressed, raises up those who are discriminated against, and chooses Mary as the blessed one. It's wonderful. There is room for anyone, even for me and you, as long as we come with empty hands, as long as we come hungry and thirsty. All those who won't come that way will go away with empty hands.

The message of the kingdom is, simultaneously, God's yes and God's no. It all depends on how you position yourself in relation to this message. Yet what surprises us is that God's no does not follow a criterion of discriminatory exclusion, but is a pronouncement against those criteria. God's no is the shadow of his yes.

What surprises us about God's yes is that it does not follow any criterion of merit. It's all-inclusive. It is based on a radical understanding of grace. And it is precisely this radical welcome—which becomes more evident the more we go to the bottom of the social pyramid—that becomes a stumbling block for people to accept and enter the kingdom. Those people simply cannot accept the fact that anyone at any time is welcomed into the kingdom, as long as he or she comes empty-handed, ready to sit down at the feet of Jesus.

Therefore, it is the radicality of God's yes that also becomes, simultaneously, a denunciation of the criteria of discrimination that our society is built on. For example, in God's kingdom there is no room for a social, economic and political practice where the place at the table of decisions, of brotherhood and of food is made according to the criteria of having (the rich), of knowing (the proud), and of power (the powerful). In the kingdom these criteria only have the virtue of calling in judgment. This is because they bring with themselves and in themselves the reality of exploitation and injustice, discrimination and humiliation, oppression and violence. They generate death not only to their victims but also to those who execute the criteria of economic, religious, or political power.

The Scriptures support this principle. We recall, for example, Jesus' encounter with the "rich young man" who, as the text says, "went away sad, because he had great wealth" (Matt. 19:22). In the second place, there is the parable of the Pharisee and the tax collector. The first man, after an arrogant prayer, went home empty-handed, for "everyone who exalts himself will be humbled" (Luke 18:14).

A third example is that of King Herod and his dramatic death, at the time of the early church: "Immediately, because Herod did not give praise to God, an angel of the Lord struck him down, and he was eaten by worms and died" (Acts 12:23).

The best way to understand the kingdom of God and how its dynamics work is to look at the life of Jesus—the things he said and did. We notice where he went and with whom he conversed. The content of the psalm, which was eloquently put into a poem, and the content of the Magnificat, which was beautifully put into a hymn, became flesh in the life of Jesus:

The Spirit of the Lord is on me, because he has anointed me to preach good news to the poor. He has sent me to proclaim freedom for the prisoners and recovery of sight for the blind, to release the oppressed, to proclaim the year of the Lord's favor. (Luke 4:18-19)

And then, on that same Sabbath day, at that synagogue in Nazareth, Jesus said, "Today this scripture is fulfilled in your hearing" (Luke 4:21).

Is there anything else we need to say? Only two options remain: surrender to discipleship or take Jesus to the hill to "throw him down the cliff," (Luke 4:29) as the people attempted to do that day. It is time for decisions in the call to discipleship.

Acts of compassion and the search for justice

The psalmist is still persistent. He keeps on the agenda the question that we avoided earlier: "What will you do with the cause of the oppressed and with the wicked ones?" Both questions are serious justice issues.

In my first reaction, I would prefer to tell him that I do not know what to do with it. It's a complex issue and I would prefer not to get into it. Yet he will not accept this kind of answer and will keep looking at me, at you, at all of us. Furthermore, there is so much of a coincidence between Psalm 146, the Magnificat and the so-called "Manifesto of Nazareth" (Luke 4:18-19) that we cannot avoid taking it seriously—very seriously.

Let me try another approach. We could say that there are two basic theological motifs that do not allow the rejection of children, the discrimination against women, the exploitation of workers, the abandonment of the elderly, and the losing of the lost. One is the compassion motif and the other one is the justice motif. Please, let's not separate them. It so happens that justice without compassion runs the risk of becoming vengeance, and compassion without a commitment to justice might even feed injustice.

Clearly, the evangelical tradition from which we come stresses the compassion motif more than the justice motif in our attempt to shape what has been called Christian social responsibility. To identify the reasons for that is a task that goes beyond this journey of ours with the psalmist and through the Magnificat. But I do want to register two comments:

1. The practice of compassion, in immediate terms—the "cup of cold water" tradition—is easier to exercise and brings some kind of immediate response: the cup of water does quench the thirst of a thirsty person.

2. The evangelical family has very often embraced a strongly unilateral concept of what should be a mature Christian relationship to authority. By advocating a theology or theory of blind submission, it has usually supported the status quo, kept silent on key justice issues, and avoided calling some wicked ones by their names. In some situations we have even denounced to the system precisely those very ones who have been engaged in the struggle for justice. In this area, we evangelicals need repentance and conversion.

On the other hand, I would like to call attention to two reasons why our commitment to justice is unavoidable. First, because it goes deep into the biblical tradition. God is a righteous God and wants justice to flourish in human relations. Nicholas

Wolterstorff takes us through a series of sharp questions so that we will face the fact that the God of justice is at the side of the poor. His commitment to justice could not have taken him to any other place:

> But why care? Why not simply teach the poor to cope? Why not praise the virtues of poverty? Why not preach a gospel of consolation as the church has done for centuries? Why try to change things? Why should poverty be on the agenda of the Christian, or of anyone else? Well, could it be that God cares? Could it be that God has taken the side of the poor?[3]

Second, our commitment to justice is unavoidable because God's love for the poor motivates and inspires it. To love the poor means to struggle for justice. Let us refer to World Vision, which as a Christian development agency has come to the conclusion that the goal of its ministry must be to go beyond development and to aim for transformation.

If we do not seriously oppose injustice and do not deliberately struggle for justice, transformation will never take place. All the efforts to overcome poverty, as well as the mechanisms and structures that generate it and are generated by it, run the risk of not going beyond being cosmetic.

The surface might even change colors, but real transformation will not be generated. Frankly speaking, I believe that much of what we have done in humanitarian help and social service has been at the cosmetic level. Time after time we have refused to get ourselves involved in the struggle for justice. To overcome this tendency, World Vision has put commitment to justice at the center of the understanding of its mission:

> World Vision is an international partnership of Christians whose mission is to follow our Lord and Savior Jesus Christ in working with the poor and oppressed to promote human transformation, seek justice and bear witness to the good news of the kingdom of God.

And what about the wicked ones? The psalmist says that God will frustrate their way. Wickedness has short legs—short life! The wicked should not forget that when the spirit departs—which is only a question of time—they will return to the ground.

We should not forget that there is an excluding interrelation between the justice of God and the wickedness of the wicked. In other words, it is because of God's commitment to justice that the song of victory of the wicked will die in their throats. It is because of God's love for the poor that the wicked, who produce so much of the poverty around us, cannot be left untouched, and wickedness cannot run its course.

It is because of the suffering and death he generates that the oppressor does not have the "right" to be a blessed one. Wickedness always generates oppression, violence and death. And God always wants peace, love and life.

In 1991, Norman Tattersall, a Canadian who worked with World Vision in Latin America, and José Chuquín, the director of World Vision in Colombia, were brutally and violently murdered in Peru. The assassin hands that mercilessly triggered the gun were never clearly identified. While the World Vision family, and the whole family of God in Latin America, were crying over the death of Norman and José, we had to include in our prayers a special petition that God would free us from hatred and from the desire for vengeance.

I must also confess that it was the death of those two brothers in Christ that brought back into my discipleship journey this dimension, that the wicked cannot walk away from God's presence unpunished. Or in the words of the psalmist, God will "frustrate the ways of the wicked."

This does not mean that God enjoys vengeance. On the contrary, to "frustrate the ways of the wicked" causes God to suffer. But love and justice, to remain love and justice, require that limits must be put on those who choose to use their lives in the service of violence, oppression and death. Those who killed Norman Tattersall and José Chuquín will not have the last word. It is Norman and José who will be dancing the dance of eternal life in the presence of the eternal God.

God's word is the last word. If it were not so, God would not be God, and the poor would have to go to sleep, day after day, without the gospel, without bread, without justice, and without the hope that a new day will arrive.

Our prayer should be that the wicked will experience conversion and find the way into discipleship. This is what remains: the invitation to follow Jesus Christ in discipleship.

The options are, by now, clear. We know who God is. We know what God does. Now it is a question of obedience. And obedience is what discipleship is all about.

Notes

1. Parul Das, "A Child's View," *World Vision* (June/July 1992): 4.

2. Donald P. Kraybill, *The Upside-Down Kingdom* (Herald Press: Scottdale, USA and Kitchener, Canada 1978), pp. 22-23.

3. Nicholas Wolterstorff, *Until Justice and Peace Embrace* (Eerdmans: Grand Rapids, 1983), p. 75.

The Lord reigns forever!

The conflict between reality and hope

PEOPLE WHO HAVE STUDIED the psalms say that they work with the presupposition that changes should occur now, within a historical framework and not in an eschatological tomorrow. "They wrestle much with the problem of the suffering of the just and the prosperity of the unjust," says John Goldingay, "and it is in this life that they expect to see justice done and oppression published."[1]

We share this expectation with the psalmist. Yet, at the level of reality, every day there are thousands of images and messages that pass before our eyes, catch our attention, move our heart and challenge our brain. What kind of world is this that we live in? What kind of hope is this that we are talking about? What kind of transformation is possible in a context like the one we face?

What do we do with Psalm 146 and with the Magnificat, our companions in this study? Can the psalmist go beyond the level of poetry? How does he establish a connection to reality? How does Mary go beyond singing when she addresses God's action in history? How and where is it possible to verify the results of that action?

A first reaction could be to say that Psalm 146 cannot be taken literally. The psalm's message is possible in a poem. Poems are like dreams and do not necessarily connect with reality. Otherwise, it is very hard to find out what to do with it. The psalmist says that "the Lord reigns forever," but frankly speaking, it is difficult to see the consequences of this in society, in the course of history. It is also difficult not to push this statement into the future and proclaim it as a dream for tomorrow. If not, how can the psalmist possibly expect "to see justice done and oppression punished today," as Goldingay says.

The psalmist, we might say, did not go to Somalia to see those children dying while the warlords dared to hinder food from reaching them. The psalmist did not visit Romania and did not hold in his arms one of those children who should not have been born—according to the Ceaucescu government—but who are alive, who come into our living rooms through a video recording as witnesses and victims of a regime that can only be described as demonic.

The psalmist did not go to Bosnia. He did not look into the eyes of one of the women whose pregnancy is the result of a massive campaign of rape inflicted by the Serbians as a war tactic. The psalmist has not been in a FEBEM home in Brazil. There, street children learn what they should not learn, and do not find what they really need. The psalmist was not in Peru. He did not see the lives of Norman and José end because of a gratuitous and irrational act of violence.

Would the psalmist still proclaim that "the Lord reigns forever," after being in Somalia and Romania, and after speaking at the funeral of Norman? All right, I do recognize that this might not be the right way to raise so many painful questions. It might be that the psalmist is the one who wants to ask the questions. He might want to ask us—you and me—whether we are willing to join him in reciting the psalm as a prayer and a confession in spite of, and in the midst of, struggles in Somalia, Brazil, in my community, and at the funeral of Norman and José. Then the psalm would become a statement of faith, a public commitment to resistance and hope, a denunciation of injustice and the auspicious announcement of a God whose commitment to justice, to the poor and the little ones is unquestionable.

To stand up at the invitation of the psalmist, and to recite the psalm again would be easier for some of us than for others. Some would go through the psalm with a joyful and loud voice affirming his or her faith in the Lord, forever.

Others would go halfway, and then the picture of a dying child would stop them in the middle—how is it that the Lord will give food to the hungry if the number of dying children, because of the lack of food, is increasing?

Others would have to breathe deeply before starting, and pray silently in their hearts with that father who brought his possessed son to Jesus and cried out "I do believe; help me overcome my unbelief" (Mark 9:24). The psalmist is not in a hurry. He will patiently wait for us to be emotionally and spiritually ready.

Are we willing to join the psalmist and pray and announce the content of this beautiful psalm in a loud voice again as a sign of hope, even if we are called to hope against hope?

Recite with me, invites the psalmist. Listen with your heart. Dream the dream of the kingdom.

> *Praise the Lord.*
> *Praise the Lord, O my soul.*
>   *I will praise the Lord all my life;*
>   *I will sing praise to my God as long as I live.*
> *Do not put your trust in princes,*
>   *in mortal men, who cannot save.*
> *When their spirit departs, they return to the ground;*
>   *on that very day their plans come to nothing.*
> *Blessed is he whose help is the God of Jacob,*
>   *whose hope is in the Lord his God,*
> *the Maker of heaven and earth,*
>   *the sea, and everything in them—*
>   *the Lord, who remains faithful forever.*

He upholds the cause of the oppressed
   and gives food to the hungry.
The Lord sets prisoners free,
   the Lord gives sight to the blind,
the Lord lifts up those who are bowed down,
   the Lord loves the righteous.
The Lord watches over the alien
   and sustains the fatherless and the widow,
   but he frustrates the ways of the wicked.
The Lord reigns forever,
   your God, O Zion, for all generations.
Praise the Lord.

What we have been saying, up to now, is crucial: How do we reconcile reality with hope, hope with reality? How do we maintain hope within the framework of history? What do we do with the psalm when we move with it from Sunday to Monday, from worship time to daily life? Can the psalm become more than a warm liturgical tool? Can it become a prayer to be transformed into a program of action? How can we possibly answer these questions? Will they not immobilize us?

Don't we feel, sometimes, as if we are breaking down from the inside out, as if it is impossible to continue to stand the dichotomy between faith and action, and hope and reality within us? Can we make the translation from the language of the sermon to the language of everyday life and the pictures of the newspaper?

As we look with the psalmist once more it seems as if what he is telling us is both complicated and simple: scream and protest, cry and lament, but do not forget to wash your face every morning in the refreshing waters of God's grace. Then walk into a new day, feeding a child, smiling to an elderly woman, planting a tree, and praying "Maranatha"— "Come, Lord Jesus."

Mary and Joseph: Can we follow their steps?

Let us invite Mary to come into the picture again. What happened to her magnificent Magnificat? You remember the day she met Elizabeth and the joy that "infected" the whole environment. It was like spring—an explosion of life: "My soul praises the Lord and my spirit rejoices in God my Savior."

Have you been there, when God seems so close, and the fellowship with brothers and sisters so warm? Have you been there when it seems as if the presence of the Spirit of God is almost palpable and you are so peaceful and so grateful for God's action and presence?

In August 1992 I participated in the Third Latin American Congress on Evangelization, in Quito, Ecuador. People from all over Latin America had come: pastors and lay people, men and women, mestizos, Indians and white folks, Quichua, Spanish and Portuguese-speaking people. When, at the close of the congress, we signed the Declaration of Quito and shared wine and bread in Holy Communion, we knew we were one and the Lord had been and was with us.

Up to the last minute we had had so many difficulties in organizing the congress. But the Lord surprised us with the wonderful gifts of fellowship and serious theological reflection, confession and reconciliation, prayer and praise, and commitment and consecration.

I was intimately involved in the whole process of organizing the event, so I felt emotionally drained and very tired at the close of the congress. Still, the awareness of God's presence was so peaceful and so palpable that I wanted to sing with Mary, "My soul praises the Lord and my spirit rejoices in God my Savior, for he has been mindful of the humble state of his servant."

But then Mary had to go home again. She had to work on her relationship with Joseph, to face her people and her community, to see her pregnancy advance and to keep struggling with some of the questions that come when you close your eyes. You don't want to let them in, but they come anyway: This pregnancy is surely strange, isn't it? Is the Lord really behind all this? Is this the way the Lord works? Will Joseph ever overcome his suspicion? Can we relate well to each other—even sexually? And what about the boy: What kind of boy will he be?

Then there was this crazy census decree. Issued by Caesar Augustus, it forced Mary and Joseph to go to Bethlehem. The decree could not have come at a worse time. After all, to harmonize an advanced pregnancy with the back of a donkey was not easy at all.

We mentioned earlier the conflict that we often have in reconciling God's revelation with our human experience, the Word with our daily life, praise with incarnated witness, hope with the daily newspaper. There is no virtue in denying this tension. It is better not to romanticize our journey in discipleship.

I believe Mary went through similar questions and tensions. After all, what is the use of the Magnificat when you cannot find a place either to rest or to deliver your baby? It would mean so much to listen to some of her stories; her many tears, her long sleepless nights, her confusion about what to do with this Jesus boy, her anger at having to go back to Jerusalem only to find him arguing theology in the temple.

How many situations were there when she did not know how to relate and how to react to Jesus: his lifestyle, the things he said and did, the people he related to, his silence and his frequent fights with Pharisees and scribes? No, it was not easy to be consistent with the promise she had made to the angel, years earlier: "May it be to me as you have said" (Luke 1:38). But at the end of the day she was one of the few who stood at the feet of the cross.

It is there that we are invited to meet her. It is there that she experiences the care of Jesus, when he says to his beloved disciple, "Here is your mother," and to Mary, "Dear woman, here is your son" (John 19:26-27). It is there that we experience his care, too—our salvation. And not least, it is there that the Magnificat acquires a new meaning and becomes the song of a new community—the community that meets at the feet of the cross:

> *My soul praises the Lord*
> > *and my spirit rejoices in God my Savior,*
> > *for he has been mindful of the humble state of his*
> > > *servant.*
> *From now on all generations will call me blessed,*
> > *for the Mighty One has done great things*
> > > *for me—*
> > *holy is his name.*
> *His mercy extends to those who fear him,*
> > *from generation to generation.*
> *He has performed mighty deeds with his arm;*
> > *he has scattered those who are proud in their*
> > > *inmost thoughts.*
> *He has brought down rulers from their thrones*
> > *but has lifted up the humble.*
> *He has filled the hungry with good things*
> > *but has sent the rich away empty.*
> *He has helped his servant Israel,*
> > *remembering to be merciful*
> *to Abraham and his descendants forever,*
> > *even as he said to our fathers.*

Poor Joseph! Blessed Joseph!

While Mary sings, Joseph is silent. While the Gospels recorded pieces of his experience, they do not register even one word that he might have spoken. He is the silent protagonist, witness and victim of this whole story.

It should not be difficult to imagine, in this "macho" culture of ours, how hard, tense and difficult it was for him to go through all this—first with Mary and this enigmatic pregnancy of hers, and then with the boy, and the strange things that happened around him.

If this whole pregnancy story was difficult for Mary, imagine what it was for Joseph! He entered this story through the back door, so to speak, and did not manage to get out again. At one point he even decided to "divorce her quietly" (Matt. 1:19).

But then came the first of a series of dreams that provided orientation to his life but never again let him sleep in peace. He might even have developed a kind of "angel syndrome." Wasn't it true that the angels came to him at night as messengers of God's revelation? Some of those visits were not easy at all.

Joseph's whole life was never again easy. To accept Mary's pregnancy, to marry her, to take her with him to Bethlehem, to witness her delivery in a very strange environment. To see these strange people come to see the boy—from the rude shepherds to the sophisticated Magi. To flee to Egypt, to come back "to the land of Israel" and finally settle down in Nazareth was not an easy journey. There were days when Joseph could not stand the tune of the Magnificat.

Still, it is this journey of obedience that makes his life so worth living. It was a life in which he seemingly lost the right to choose his own options and to establish his goals, but it became a central piece in the kingdom movement. There are three elements in Joseph's experience to which I want to call attention:

a) *The strange privilege of being used by God.*

As we have already seen, Joseph was a quiet man. All he wanted in life was to work as a carpenter, get married, establish a family, and live in peace in his community. But God messed it all up. Yet is this not my story and your story, too? Maybe with fewer colors, but still a common story for those who follow Jesus.

Joseph's life would never be the same after the angel visited him for the first time. Our lives will never be the same after we receive the call to begin a journey that sometimes looks so difficult, so strange and so hard to understand. But it is this sense of calling that gives meaning to our lives and keeps us going, isn't it?

If we look back at Joseph's story and our own story, we will always conclude that it is God's calling that gives meaning to our lives. It was God himself who provided, step by step, revelation by revelation, the orientation we needed to shape our journey of obedience to his message and the reality of the kingdom of God. Mary is right as she tries to give meaning to her life in the light of God's promises to his people:

> He has helped his servant Israel,
>   remembering to be merciful
> to Abraham and his descendants forever,
>   even as he said to our fathers.

Joseph was a man whose life was profoundly

changed by his vocation to be at the service of the kingdom. It was precisely this experience that gave meaning to his life.

b) *The courage to obey.*

It is very interesting to notice what Joseph's reaction was after he received one of those conflictive but revealing visits from an angel. "When Joseph woke up, he did what the angel of the Lord had commanded him" (Matt. 1:24).

Simple obedience was Joseph's response, time after time. And it was this simple obedience that kept him going. From revelation to obedience is a good way to go, even when it is hard to accept.

Mary had the virtue of finding graceful language to describe those kinds of encounters with God's revelation. After the angel told her what would happen to her, she said "I am the Lord's servant . . . May it be to me as you have said" (Luke 1:38).

Are we still ready for this kind of fresh, even if costly, obedience? It is this obedience that keeps us young even when we are growing old.

c) *On the way to Nazareth.*

Joseph, the silent man, did not understand (I presume) everything that was happening with him and around him. He might not have understood much. Yet the secret of his life was that he kept obeying, and at the end of the story he be-came known as a man at the service of the kingdom:

> and he went and lived in a town called Nazareth.
> So was fulfilled what was said through the prophets:
> "He [Jesus] will be called a Nazarene." (Matt. 2:23)

Joseph was, in his time and in his context, a man at the service of the kingdom. This is why we are evoking his experience and establishing him as a model to be followed.

How will our own life and options be described tomorrow? What will be said about us tomorrow depends on the directions we will give to our lives today. Today is the time to say "yes" to God's revelations. Today is the time to place our lives at the service of the kingdom of God.

It would be very interesting to sit at the feet of Joseph and Mary and listen to their stories—the events and experiences, the struggles and joys of people who had their lives reoriented by their calling to serve the kingdom. Since we cannot do this, we can recall to memory the stories of our lives and try to discern the directions we are taking and the goals we are reaching: Are we following in the steps of the Nazarene?

When I think about my life I conclude that I could never have dreamed of the directions it is taking. If my parents had wanted to direct my life in this way they would not have succeeded at all. Growing up in a city with a strong German influence in southern Brazil, they did not even have the categories to dream about such a life, even if they wanted to.

It was the gospel that gave meaning to my life. It was God's calling that gave direction to my existence. It was the cause of the kingdom of God that set me on a journey, on a kind of pilgrimage in discipleship. Since then I have been unable to settle down.

While I was single my parents would say, again and again, "Why don't you stay here?" I suspect they knew I would not—that I just could not. These days, it is my wife who would like me to stay at home a few more days. Yet by facing the temptation that says "Why don't you cancel this or that?" she knows in her heart that I can't, and somehow keeps silent. Both of us rejoice with every trip that ends in her arms. My children? I do not know yet if they will understand.

The basic drive that should motivate all our stories is to place ourselves at the service of the kingdom. Joseph fulfilled his part. Mary even sang about her part: "From now on all generations will call me blessed, for the Mighty One has done great things for me—holy is his name."

As for all of us, it may be time to learn with another Mary who was also chosen to be with the Lord, because she, too, had made the right choice: "Mary has chosen what is better, and it will not be taken away from her." (Luke 10:42).

The "little ones" set the agenda

We are coming to the end of this talk between Mary, the psalmist and us. It was set up as a chat among disciples. The kingdom of God has been the central biblical idea around which we have been sitting. We have stressed the centrality and the importance of the kingdom because Jesus did so, and because the poor call us to do so. What emerges from this whole process is an invitation to discipleship. This is the point of departure and arrival in the kingdom.

As we come to the close of our journey, I'd like to evoke a final biblical image.

In the tenth chapter of his gospel, Luke tells us about the experience of a group of 72 disciples that Jesus sent out, two by two, on a mission. When they returned they were happy and felt proud about themselves, as we often do when we come back from a successful journey. They had experienced powerful things and, as they said, "even the demons submit to us in your name" (Luke 10:17).

Then something surprising happened, as it so often does in our kingdom involvement. Jesus takes charge of the conversation and turns everything around.

First, he tells them that he knew about their experiences as well as about their authority over the demons. In fact, it was Jesus who gave them such authority. Then he tells them that the reason for their happiness should be another one: "However, do not rejoice that the spirits submit to you, but rejoice that your names are written in heaven" (Luke 10:20). The demons still need to be rebuked, but at the end of the day, what really matters is to be known by God.

Are we ready and willing to live with that? To give our best to the cause of the kingdom, as Mary did, and be happy because we are "known by God"?

Our job description may be impressive, the quality of our work commendable, the impact of our ministry recognized by many, even the depth and intensity of our spiritual authority might be felt by all, but what really matters is that we faithfully follow the steps of Jesus in obedient discipleship. "Blessed is he whose help is the God of Jacob, whose hope is in the Lord his God," says the psalmist.

Second, Jesus starts to speak, joyfully, about little children, and reveals to that group of disciples a central dimension of the kingdom of God:

> At that time Jesus, full of joy through the Holy Spirit, said, "I praise you, Father, Lord of heaven and earth, because you have hidden these things

from the wise and learned, and revealed them to little children. Yes, Father, for this was your good pleasure" (Luke 10:21).

It really sounds crazy, doesn't it? How can it be that the secrets of the kingdom of God are placed in the hands of "little children?" Although it sounds strange, it also looks kingdom-like.

In one way or another, this is what this whole book is all about. The kingdom of God is so surprisingly different to make it absolutely clear that it is in God's hands, and because it is in God's hands it is surprisingly different. Only as a surprise can we take part in it. Mary herself went through this experience: "for he has been mindful of the humble state of his servant."

No, I do not think Jesus is talking only about little children. I think he is talking about people with empty hands, the little ones, the poor, the sick, the oppressed. He is talking about and to disciples:

Then he turned to his disciples and said privately, "Blessed are the eyes that see what you see. For I tell you that many prophets and kings wanted to see what you see but did not see it, and to hear what you hear but did not hear it." (Luke 10:23-24)

The challenge the disciples faced is our challenge too: To boast about the results of our success and missionary journeys and be "unknown" by God, or to live from and in a constant state of surprise for having the privilege of drinking from the secrets of the kingdom of God, in and through Jesus Christ.

By looking at the little ones we will know which way to go. They establish the agenda. If we do not follow this track, all our strategies and priorities, in the language of the psalmist, will "return to the ground." Jesus can be dramatic about all this:

> *He took a little child and had him stand among them. Taking him in his arms, he said to them, "Whoever welcomes one of these little children in my name welcomes me; and whoever welcomes me does not welcome me but the one who sent me." (Mark 9:36-37)*

So we come to the end of this conversation, grateful for the company of the psalmist and the richness of the Magnificat.

The beauty, the challenge and the invitation to share the secrets and live out the reality of the kingdom of God amazes and surprises us. I am silent!

Humbly I sit down. And happily I go on.

I am silent so I can listen and receive. Being silent does not mean giving up the struggle and the dream. Those are a gift, too. The legitimacy of the struggle depends on our humble willingness to obey and to serve. It depends on our willingness to receive the "little ones" and to receive from them. Silence means the willingness to learn with Mary, to "treasure all these things" in our hearts (Luke 2:51).

I must prostrate myself humbly, because the kingdom identifies no one according to the criteria of success, merit, dedication or effort. In the kingdom it is necessary to learn how to receive and to give. It's all a question of grace and discipleship.

And I go on joyfully because grace sustains us. The invitation to follow Jesus gives meaning to our lives and purpose to our journey. This is a worthy way to live. As the psalmist would say, "Praise the Lord."

Notes

1. John Goldingay, "The Message of Psalms," in *The Message of the Bible* (Lion Book: Tring, England, Batavia, USA, Sydney, Australia, 1988), p. 76.